FRANCIS FRITH'S
EDINBURGH
PHOTOGRAPHIC MEMORIES

HAWTHORNDEN, FROM THE GLEN 1897 39161

EDINBURGH

PHOTOGRAPHIC MEMORIES

CLIVE HARDY

First published as Edinburgh, Photographic Memories
in 1998 by WBC Ltd
Revised paperback edition published in the United Kingdom in 2000 by
The Frith Book Company as Edinburgh, Photographic Memories
This edition published in the United Kingdom in 2005 by
The Francis Frith Collection®
ISBN 1-85937-193-0

British Library Cataloguing in Publication Data

Edinburgh
Photographic Memories
Clive Hardy

The Francis Frith Collection®
Frith's Barn, Teffont,
Salisbury, Wiltshire SP3 5QP
Tel: +44 (0) 1722 716 376
Email: info@francisfrith.co.uk
www.francisfrith.co.uk

Aerial photographs reproduced under licence from Simmons Aerofilms Limited
Historical Ordnance Survey maps reproduced under licence from Homecheck.co.uk

Printed and bound in England

Front Cover: EDINBURGH, PRINCES STREET, WEST END 1897 39113t
The colour-tinting in this image is for illustrative purposes only,
and is not intended to be historically accurate

Every attempt has been made to contact copyright holders of illustrative material.
We will be happy to give full acknowledgement in future editions for any items not
credited. Any information should be directed to The Francis Frith Collection.

AS WITH ANY HISTORICAL DATABASE, THE FRANCIS FRITH ARCHIVE IS CONSTANTLY BEING
CORRECTED AND IMPROVED, AND THE PUBLISHERS WOULD WELCOME INFORMATION ON
OMISSIONS OR INACCURACIES

EDINBURGH
PHOTOGRAPHIC MEMORIES

CONTENTS

THE MAKING OF AN ARCHIVE

Francis Frith, Victorian founder of the world-famous photographic archive, was a devout Quaker and a highly successful Victorian businessman. By 1860 he was already a multi-millionaire, having established and sold a wholesale grocery business in Liverpool. He had also made a series of pioneering photographic journeys to the Nile region. The images he returned with were the talk of London. An eminent modern historian has likened their impact on the population of the time to that on our own generation of the first photographs taken on the surface of the moon.

Frith had a passion for landscape, and was as equally inspired by the countryside of Britain as he was by the desert regions of the Nile. He resolved to set out on a new career and to use his skills with a camera. He established a business in Reigate as a specialist publisher of topographical photographs.

Frith lived in an era of immense and sometimes violent change. For the poor in the early part of Victoria's reign work was a drudge and the hours long, and ordinary people had precious little free time. Most had not travelled far beyond the boundaries of their own town or village. Mass tourism was in its infancy during the 1860s, but during the next decade the railway network and the establishment of Bank Holidays and half-Saturdays gradually made it possible for the working man and his family to enjoy holidays and to see a little more of the world. With characteristic business acumen, Francis Frith foresaw that these new tourists would enjoy having souvenirs to commemorate their days out. He began selling photo-souvenirs of seaside resorts and beauty spots, which the Victorian public pasted into treasured family albums.

Frith's aim was to photograph every town and village in Britain. For the next thirty years he travelled the country by train and by pony and trap, producing fine photographs of seaside resorts and beauty spots that were keenly bought by millions of Victorians.

THE RISE OF FRITH & CO

Each photograph was taken with tourism in mind, the small team of Frith photographers concentrating on busy shopping streets, beaches, seafronts, picturesque lanes and villages. They also photographed buildings: the Victorian and Edwardian eras were times of huge building activity, and town halls, libraries, post offices, schools and technical colleges were springing up all over the country. They were invariably celebrated by a proud Victorian public, and photo souvenirs – visual records – published by F Frith & Co were sold in their hundreds of thousands. In addition, many new commercial buildings such as hotels, inns and pubs were photographed, often because their owners specifically commissioned Frith postcards or prints of them for re-sale or for publicity purposes.

In order to gain some understanding of the scale of Frith's business one only has to look at the catalogue issued by Frith & Co in 1886: it runs to some 670 pages. By 1890 Frith had created the greatest specialist photographic publishing company in the world, with over 2,000 stockists! The picture on the right shows the Frith & Co display board on the wall of the stockist at Ingleton in the Yorkshire Dales (left of window). Beautifully constructed with a mahogany frame and gilt inserts, it displayed a dozen scenes.

Postcard Bonanza

The ever-popular holiday postcard we know today took many years to appear, and F Frith & Co was in the vanguard of its development. Postcards became a hugely popular means of communication and sold in their millions. Frith's company took full advantage of this boom and soon became the major publisher of photographic view postcards.

Francis Frith died in 1898 at his villa in Cannes, his great project still growing. His sons Eustace and Cyril continued their father's monumental task, expanding the number of views offered to the public and recording more and more places in Britain, as the coasts and countryside were opened up to mass travel. The archive Frith created continued in business for another seventy years. By 1970 it contained over a third of a million pictures of 7,000 cities, towns and villages. The massive photographic record Frith has left to us stands as a living monument to a special and very remarkable man.

This book shows Edinburgh as it was photographed by this world-famous archive at various periods in its development over the past 150 years. Every photograph was taken for a specific commercial purpose, which explains why the selection may not show every aspect of the city landscape. However, the photographs, compiled from one of the world's most celebrated archives, provide an important and absorbing record of Edinburgh.

EDINBURGH FROM THE AIR 1929   AF27136

LINLITHGOW

Situated approximately half-way between Stirling and Edinburgh, Linlithgow became an important and favourite royal residence. During the wars with the English, the town and its castle were subject to siege and counter-siege. At Lent in 1314 the English took Linlithgow by blocking the fall of its portcullis with hay-carts. Edward II hurried through the town on his way to Dunbar and the safety of a ship, following his defeat at Bannockburn.

LINLITHGOW PALACE 1897 39155

The last Scottish national parliament was held here in 1646. Oliver Cromwell lived at the palace for several months following the Battle of Dunbar in September 1650.

LINLITHGOW

LINLITHGOW PALACE, FROM THE BOAT STATION 1897 39153

King David I built the first manor house at Linlithgow, and the church of St Michael next to it. In 1301, Edward Longshanks set about rebuilding and heavily fortifying the palace, and it was held by the English until the autumn of 1313.

LINLITHGOW PALACE, QUEEN MARGARET'S BOWER 1897 39156

The royal apartments were situated on the west side of the quadrangle.

Queen Margaret's Bower is where her majesty kept vigil while James IV fought at Flodden.

LINLITHGOW

LINLITHGOW PALACE, ON THE
SOUTH SHORE OF LINLITHGOW
LOCH 1897 39154

Mary, Queen of Scots was born here in
1542, and Prince Charles Edward Stuart
stayed here in 1745. The palace is thought
to have been burnt down accidentally in
1746 by some of General Hawley's troops.

LINLITHGOW, THE CHURCH AND THE PALACE 1897 39158

Founded by David I in the 12th century, the church was rebuilt about 300 years later.

LINLITHGOW

LINLITHGOW, THE CROSS WELL 1897 39157

This well, with its thirteen water jets, is a reconstruction of an earlier one destroyed by Oliver Cromwell's troops. On 23 January 1570, Regent Moray was shot as he rode through Linlithgow. The assassin hid in a house belonging to John Hamilton, Archbishop of St Andrews. Moray's friends hanged Hamilton at Stirling in 1571. They did not go to the expense of a trial.

QUEENSFERRY

The town of Queensferry lies on the south shore of the Firth of Forth. South Queensferry and its counterpart North Queensferry are said have been so-named because Queen Margaret crossed the Forth at this point on her way to Dunfermline.

THE FORTH RAILWAY BRIDGE C1890 558

Designed by Sir John Fowler and Sir Benjamin Baker, the Forth Bridge cost £3,000,000 to build. Of the workforce of 4,500 men, 57 were killed in work-related accidents.

Queensferry

THE FORTH BRIDGE 1897 39142

Construction of the bridge commenced in November 1882. The first test trains ran from
January 1890, and the official opening took place on 4 March 1890.

THE FORTH BRIDGE 1897 39141

The bridge is more than over 2,760 yards long, including the approach viaducts, giving a clear headway at high water of 150 ft.
The steel towers stand 360 ft high and are supported on granite piers. The deepest foundations are 88 ft below high water.

QUEENSFERRY

THE VIEW FROM NORTH QUEENSFERRY 1897 39144

Following the opening of the Forth Bridge, the North British
Railway Co decided that they could dispense with their ferry
services. Accordingly, the licences for the Forth and the Tay were
transferred to David Wilson & Sons.

Newhaven

The fishermen's wives were
known for their costumes,
which are thought to have
had associations with the
community's Scandinavian
origins. The women also
had their own cries when
selling fish: 'Caller Herrin'
(fresh herrings) and 'Caller
Ou' (fresh oysters).

NEWHAVEN

The small fishing port of Newhaven was founded by James IV in about 1500. A shipyard and ropeworks were established for the construction of warships.

LEFT: NEWHAVEN, THE HARBOUR FROM HAWTHORNDEN 1897 39138

In about 1512, one of the biggest warships then in existence was fitting out at Newhaven. She was 'The Great Michael; she was 240 ft long, and carried a crew of 420 and 1,000 soldiers. The mighty warship was one of the units despatched by James IV to assist the French against Henry VIII.

NEWHAVEN, THE HARBOUR 1897 39139

The original population of Newhaven was probably of Dutch and Scandinavian origin. For generations the people rarely moved out of their own community, keeping their traditions and customs alive.

EDINBURGH

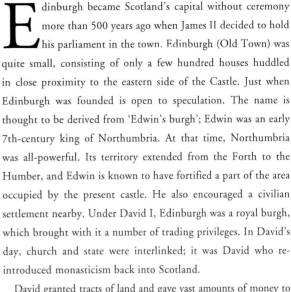

EDINBURGH, JOHN KNOX'S HOUSE 1897 39125

This view shows the lower reach of the High Street looking towards Canongate. The building immediately behind the lamp standard is known as John Knox's house. Dating from the 16th century, the house is said to have been built by the goldsmith of Mary, Queen of Scots. Just how long Knox lived here is open to debate.

Edinburgh became Scotland's capital without ceremony more than 500 years ago when James II decided to hold his parliament in the town. Edinburgh (Old Town) was quite small, consisting of only a few hundred houses huddled in close proximity to the eastern side of the Castle. Just when Edinburgh was founded is open to speculation. The name is thought to be derived from 'Edwin's burgh'; Edwin was an early 7th-century king of Northumbria. At that time, Northumbria was all-powerful. Its territory extended from the Forth to the Humber, and Edwin is known to have fortified a part of the area occupied by the present castle. He also encouraged a civilian settlement nearby. Under David I, Edinburgh was a royal burgh, which brought with it a number of trading privileges. In David's day, church and state were interlinked; it was David who re-introduced monasticism back into Scotland.

David granted tracts of land and gave vast amounts of money to the greater glory of God, encouraging Benedictines, Cistercians and most of all Augustinians, to found religious houses. The legend goes that David was out hunting when he was attacked by an infuriated stag. He was saved from certain death by the interposition of a miraculous cross. In thanks, and as a penance for hunting on a holy day, David founded an abbey at Holyrood. Despite the foundation of a great abbey, much of Edinburgh's early history appears to revolve around the castle and the fortunes of the monarchy. Henry VIII was desperate for his son Edward, aged five, to be married to the infant Queen Mary. Scotland at that time was under the governorship of James, 2nd Earl of Arran, who was a Protestant. Through argument, coercion, and downright bribery, Arran persuaded the Scottish parliament to agree to the match, and it was ratified in two treaties at Holyrood in August 1543. But Scotland, as so often in the past, was in turmoil. Mary of Guise, the infant Queen's mother, was against the wedding; she had the backing of a number of nobles and the Catholic Church. For some reason, Arran suddenly changed faiths and sides, and the infant was crowned Queen of the Scots. Henry was not impressed. In May 1544, an English invasion force arrived off Newhaven. Edinburgh fell to the troops of the Earl of Hertford, though the castle managed to hold out. Hertford burnt Holyroodhouse and the Old Town.

The following year, Hertford was back in Scotland, burning five market towns, sacking 243 villages, and laying waste to crops.

23

EDINBURGH

Edward VI of England was destined not marry the Queen of Scots. He died in 1553 and was succeeded by his Catholic sister. The young Scottish queen was married to Francois, Dauphin of France, an act that was to establish the Auld Alliance. The marriage lasted two years. By 1560 Francois too was dead, and Mary had returned to Scotland.

EDINBURGH, HOLYROOD PALACE,
KING CHARLES'S BEDROOM 1897 39173

ABOVE: EDINBURGH,
HOLYROOD PALACE AND
ARTHUR'S SEAT 1897 39168

Extensive alterations to the palace
were undertaken between 1670
and 1679 by Sir William Bruce,
the king's surveyor in Scotland.
The strong French influence in
Sir William's designs reflected
Charles II's passion for things
Gallic.

LEFT: EDINBURGH, HOLYROOD
PALACE, KING CHARLES'S
BEDROOM 1897 39172

A fence and rope guard the old
feathered four-poster bed, with the
once elaborate canopy and drapes,
giving the bed a majestic air.

EDINBURGH

ABOVE: EDINBURGH, HOLYROOD PALACE, THE FRONT ENTRANCE 1897 39169

The building of Holyroodhouse was started in about 1500 by James IV; the work continued under James V, who added a new tower and quadrangle. In May 1544, the palace was badly damaged when it was set on fire by the Earl of Hertford's troops.

LEFT: EDINBURGH, HOLYROOD PALACE, THE CHAPEL FRONT 1897 39170

This photograph shows the Chapel Royal at Holyroodhouse. It was originally the nave of the abbey founded in 1128 by David I.

ABOVE: EDINBURGH, HOLYROOD PALACE, THE REMAINS OF THE CHAPEL ROYAL 1897 39171

The chapel was the burial place of David II, James II and James V. The chapel was sacked during the revolution of 1688, but the real damage was done in 1768 when the roof collapsed.

RIGHT: EDINBURGH, ST GILES'S CATHEDRAL 1897 39126

The High Kirk of St Giles was largely built in the 14th and 15th centuries. The tower, which dates from c1495, is topped off with what is considered to be the finest example of a crown steeple in the whole of Scotland.

EDINBURGH

ABOVE: EDINBURGH, THE CANONGATE TOLBOOTH C1890 E24503

The Canongate was where the canons of Holyrood Abbey entered the Old Town. The tolbooth, with its projecting clock, is one of the most famous landmarks on the Royal Mile and dates from 1591.

BELOW: EDINBURGH, THE CANONGATE TOLBOOTH 1897 39124A

In the great days of the Old Town, Canongate Street was where members of the Scottish aristocracy had their town houses.

ABOVE: EDINBURGH, HOLYROOD PALACE AND ARTHUR'S SEAT C1900 E24502

The dominating mass of Arthur's seat, 822 ft high, stands in a 648-acre park.

In 1634, Charles I attempted to re-establish the Scottish Episcopal Church, and St Giles's was for a short period elevated to the status of a cathedral. It became a cathedral again under Charles II, only to revert to being a parish church in 1688.

EDINBURGH

EDINBURGH, ST GILES'S
CATHEDRAL 1897
39129

The oldest parish church
in Edinburgh, St Giles's
was erected in the early
12th century on the site
of an older building. In
1385, much of the church
was badly damaged by fire,
and the rebuilding was not
completed until 1460.

EDINBURGH, ST GILES'S
CATHEDRAL 1897
39128

During the Reformation,
the interior of the church
was defaced, and altars
and relics were destroyed.
In 1559, John Knox was
appointed minister of St
Giles's. The building was
in fact divided into four
separate churches, and
remained so until the 19th
century.

EDINBURGH

EDINBURGH, ST GILES'S
CATHEDRAL, THE TOMB
OF THE MARQUIS OF
MONTROSE 1897
39130

In 1644, James Graham,
5th Earl of Montrose,
raised an army to fight for
King Charles I. Against
all odds, Montrose gained
victory after victory until
his luck finally ran out at
Philliphaugh in September
1645. Montrose escaped to
the Continent, but returned
to raise troops for Charles II.
Betrayed to the Covenanters,
he was hung, drawn and
quartered at Edinburgh on
21 May 1650.

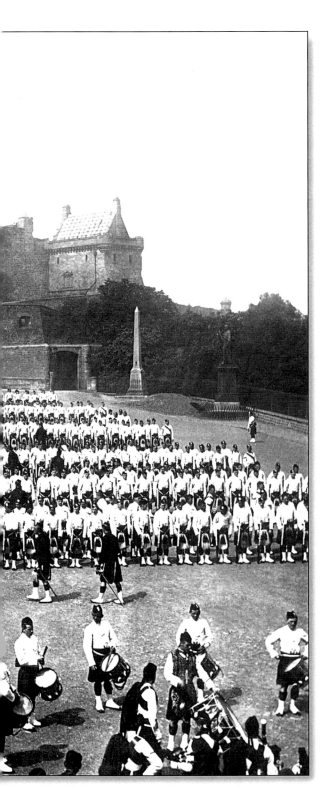

EDINBURGH, THE CASTLE 1897 39121A

A battalion of the Black Watch parade on the castle esplanade. Raised by General Wade in 1725, the Black Watch was formally constituted as a regiment of the line in 1739, and its strength was increased from four to ten companies.

EDINBURGH

EDINBURGH, THE CASTLE FROM
THE GRASSMARKET 1883 E24303

The grassmarket was the scene in 1736 of the Porteous
Riots. A temporary gallows had been erected for the
execution of Andrew Wilson for smuggling. Captain 'Black
Jock' Porteous was in command of the city guard that took
Wilson to his execution. A disturbance broke out, and
Porteous ordered his men to open fire on the crowd.
He was later arrested, tried and condemned to death; but
because of the circumstances of the case, a stay of execution
was granted until the king returned from Hanover. There
were many people in Edinburgh who hated Porteous;
fearing that he would be pardoned, a mob broke into
the jail, hauled him off to the Grassmarket and
lynched him. Despite the offering of a large reward
for information, no one was ever charged with
Porteous's murder.

EDINBURGH

EDINBURGH

EDINBURGH, THE CASTLE FROM JOHNSTON TERRACE 1897 39120

During the reign of James III, the king's brothers were imprisoned here on suspicion of conspiring against him. John, Earl of Mar, died in Craigmillar Castle after being over-bled whilst suffering from a fever. Alexander, Duke of Albany, managed to kill his gaolers and escaped down a rope made of sheets.

LEFT: EDINBURGH, THE CASTLE, THE CANNON 'MONS MEG' c1950 E24001

The cannon 'Mons Meg' is said to have been cast at Mons, Belgium in 1486, on the orders of James III. When James IV came to use the brute at the siege of Norham Castle in 1497, it took an artillery train of 220 men and 90 horses to get 'Mons Meg' to the scene of the action.

BELOW: EDINBURGH, THE CASTLE FROM PRINCES GARDENS 1897 39119

The gardens, the railway line and Princes Street occupy the area once covered by the waters of Nor' Loch. The loch and an area of marshland formed a part of the castle's defences, but they also inhibited Edinburgh's expansion. The decision was taken in the 1770s to drain the loch and marshland to allow the development of the New Town.

RIGHT: EDINBURGH, THE CASTLE AND THE NATIONAL GALLERY 1897 E24506

The Edinburgh Castle we see today is, with a few additions, that built by the Earl of Morton following the siege of 1572. Morton succeeded Lennox as Regent, and took the fortress in the name of the infant James VI from the supporters of Mary, Queen of Scots. It was Morton who added the great half-moon battery to the castle's defences.

EDINBURGH

EDINBURGH

EDINBURGH, THE CASTLE
FROM THE GRASSMARKET
1897 39121

The site of the Marquis of
Montrose's execution was not
here, but at the Mercat Cross
in the High Street. Having
been declared a traitor in 1644,
Montrose was not given the ben-
efit of a trial. After hanging for
three hours, his body was taken
down and quartered. His head
was set upon the tolbooth, and
his limbs were sent for public
display on the gates of Stirling,
Glasgow, Perth and Aberdeen.
In 1661, Montrose was allowed a
state burial.

EDINBURGH

EDINBURGH, A VIEW FROM THE CASTLE 1897 39101

In the foreground are the buildings of the Royal Institute and the National Gallery, with Princes Street on the left behind the Scott Monument. Calton Hill can be seen in the distance.

EDINBURGH, THE CITY AND THE FIRTH OF FORTH C1950 E24003

A tramcar rattles over the junction of Frederick Street and Princes Street. Edinburgh was well served by its tramway system for 85 years; services came to an end in November 1956.

EDINBURGH, THE UNIVERSITY 1897 39134

Edinburgh University was founded by James VI in 1582. The buildings we see in this photograph were constructed between 1789 and 1827, and the dome was added in 1887. By the early years of the 20th century, the university had 3,000 students, 40 professors, 43 lecturers and 44 examiners.

EDINBURGH, A VIEW FROM THE CASTLE C1950 E24004

A similar view to photograph No 39101, page 40, but separated in time by 50 years.

LEFT: EDINBURGH, DONALDSON'S
HOSPITAL 1897 39136

The hospital was erected and endowed
for the maintenance and education of
up to 300 children, of whom 100 had
speech and/or hearing difficulties. The
benefactor was a wealthy printer who
died in 1880, leaving £200,000 for the
project.

ABOVE: EDINBURGH, HERIOT'S HOSPITAL 1897 39135

George Heriot, goldsmith and banker to James VI, founded the hospital. He was immortalised as Jingling Geordie in Walter Scott's 'Fortunes of Nigel'. Construction began on the hospital in 1628, but it was not completed until 1693 when it saw service as a military hospital.

BELOW: EDINBURGH, THE INFIRMARY 1897 39133

Built in the Scottish Baronial style, at a cost of £400,000, the infirmary was dealing with 8,000 patients a year by 1900.

ABOVE: EDINBURGH, THE MUSEUM OF ANTIQUITIES 1897 39115

Founded in 1823, this building, at the foot of The Mound, housed a statue gallery when this picture was taken. There was also a collection of casts that was open only to art students.

EDINBURGH

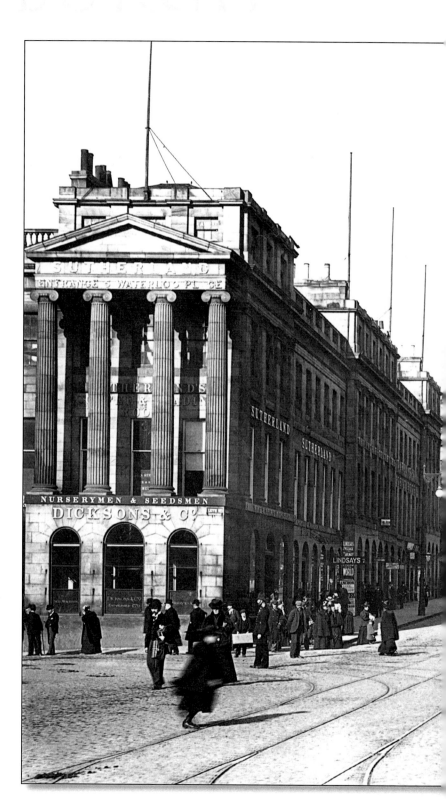

**EDINBURGH, WATERLOO PLACE
1897 39117**

In the background on Calton Hill
stands the unfinished monument to the
Scottish dead of the Napoleonic Wars.
The monument was started in 1822,
but the money ran out and it was never
completed.

EDINBURGH

BELOW: EDINBURGH, THE MUSEUM AND CASTLE C1900 E24509

The magnificent entrance to the Royal Institution.

LEFT: EDINBURGH, FROM CALTON HILL 1897 39103A

In the foreground is the castellated bulk of the prison. The old Calton burial ground just beyond is where the philosopher David Hume is buried.

EDINBURGH, PRINCES STREET, LOOKING WEST 1897 39107

It was possible to keep healthy on Princes Street. The Edinburgh Cafe at number 70 did not serve alcohol, and there was a Turkish baths at number 90. For those with a sweet tooth, Edinburgh rock was available at Ferguson's.

EDINBURGH, THE NATIONAL GALLERY 1897 39106

The collection included paintings of the Spanish and Italian Schools, and the British were represented by artists such as Gainsborough. The annual Exhibition of the Scottish Academy was one of the highlights of the year.

EDINBURGH, WATERLOO PLACE
1897 39116

On the left is the Register House
containing the Scottish archives.
Over on the right is the general post
office. The statue is of the Duke of
Wellington.

EDINBURGH

EDINBURGH

EDINBURGH,
THE SCOTT
MONUMENT
1897 39112

In this view of the
Scott Monument,
we can see in the
foreground a nanny
enjoying a well earned
rest.

EDINBURGH, PRINCES STREET AND THE SCOTT MONUMENT 1897 39112A

Note the cabs and brakes alongside the Scott Monument. During the summer, excursions could be taken from here to the Forth Bridge and Queensferry and also to Roslin.

EDINBURGH, PRINCES STREET AND THE SCOTT MONUMENT c1900 F24504

Princes Street and the Scott Monument from the gardens.

EDINBURGH

EDINBURGH, PRINCES
STREET 1897 39108

At the turn of the 20th
century Princes Street boasted
a number of hotels. The most
expensive to stay at was the
North British at Waverley
Station. Next on the list were
the Caledonian, the Station
and the Royal, followed by
the somewhat cheaper Royal
British, the Douglas and the
Bedford. There was also the
Old Waverley, which was a
temperance establishment.

EDINBURGH, PRINCES
STREET, WEST END 1897
39113

Considered to be one of the
finest boulevards in Europe,
Princes Street was the place
to shop and eat. Restaurants
included a branch of Ferguson
& Forrester, the Royal British,
and Littlejohn's. Confectioners
included Mackies, and also
Ritchies, where shortbread was
a speciality.

EDINBURGH

EDINBURGH
PRINCES STREET 1897 39114

This photograph shows the junction of Hope Street, Queensferry Street and Sandwick Street. St John's and St Cuthbert's Churches, along with the castle, provide the backdrop.

EDINBURGH, THE SCOTT MONUMENT AND PRINCES STREET GARDENS c1875 E24510

The monument was designed by George Kemp and built between 1840 and 1844. Scott owned several houses in the city: the most famous was 39 Castle Street, where he wrote many of the Waverley novels.

EDINBURGH, WAVERLEY STATION 1883 E24302

The platform canopies were still under construction when this photograph was taken. The station was originally called North Bridge, but it was renamed in April 1866.

EDINBURGH, PRINCES GARDENS 1897 39122

This view of Princes Gardens looks towards The Mound.

EDINBURGH

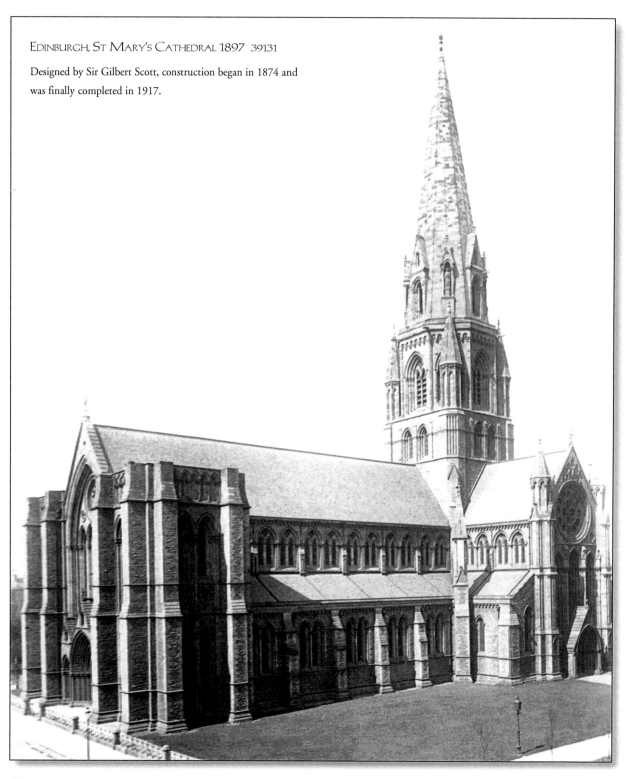

EDINBURGH, ST MARY'S CATHEDRAL 1897 39131

Designed by Sir Gilbert Scott, construction began in 1874 and
was finally completed in 1917.

EDINBURGH, ST MARY'S CATHEDRAL 1897   39132

Here we see the imposing interior of St Mary's Cathedral. By 1879, construction costs amounted to more than £110,000.

ROSLIN

Roslin is famous for its castle and chapel. The oldest part of the castle, which was founded by Sir William Sinclair, dates from the early 14th century. The consecration of the chapel was delayed because a murder had been committed on the premises by the chief stonemason.

ROSLIN CHAPEL 1897 39164

The chapel, which is famed for its elaborate carvings, was founded in 1446 as a collegiate church, but only the lady chapel and choir were completed. The church was badly damaged by rioters in 1688 and was restored in the 19th century.

ROSLIN

The castle stands on a cliff above the river North Esk. The oldest part dates from the early 14th century. It was enlarged in the 1440s.

All but destroyed in 1544 during an English invasion, the castle was rebuilt by 1580. Further additions were made during the 17th century.

RIGHT: ROSLIN CHAPEL, INTERIOR 1897 39164A

The chapel is famed for its pillar of entwined ribbands. The story is that the chief stonemason went to Italy to study a similar pillar. While he was away, his apprentice worked out how to construct the pillar after having a dream and built it. On his return, the mason was so jealous of his apprentice's work that he struck the boy dead.

BELOW: ROSLIN CASTLE, PART OF THE OLD RUINS 1897 39165

The castle and church have long been popular with tourists, many of whom stay to sample the delights of the Old Rosslyn Inn. Among those to imbibe have been Johnson and Boswell in 1773, Robert Burns, Queen Victoria and Edward VII.

HAWTHORNDEN

Located nine miles south of Edinburgh, Hawthornden stands high above the river North Esk amid a densely wooded estate. The home of the poet William Drummond (1585-1649), the house was extensively rebuilt by him in 1638.

HAWTHORNDEN 1897 39159

The English poet laureate Ben Jonson stayed here from December 1618 until the middle of January 1619 as a guest of William Drummond.

Hawthornden

Hawthornden, From the Glen 1897 39161

A picturesque view of Hawthornden.

HAWTHORNDEN

HAWTHORNDEN THE COURTYARD 1897 39163

Jonson was 45 years old when in 1618 he left London and walked the 400 miles to Scotland. At Darlington his shoes gave out, and he had to buy another pair. He later told Drummond that they took some breaking in and left his feet sore and blistered for several days.

HAWTHORNDEN, BEN JONSON'S TREE 1897 39162

It is said that Drummond was sitting under the great sycamore tree in front of the house when Jonson trudged up the path. Drummond met him with 'Welcome, welcome, royal Ben!' Jonson replied: 'Thank ye, thank ye, Hawthornden! Drummond's library was one of the finest of its day, containing about 1,400 books in English, French, Latin, Greek, Spanish, Italian and Hebrew.

NORTH BERWICK

It was at North Berwick, in 1591, that the devil is said to have appeared to a group of witches in St Andrew's Kirk. At their trial for witchcraft, the women confessed that they not only knew the most intimate secrets of the king's bedchamber, but that their satanic leader was none other than Francis Stewart, Earl of Bothwell. Bothwell, though well-educated, was probably mad, and not afraid of using violence. The king, who believed in witchcraft, ordered Bothwell's arrest. Bothwell escaped from custody and crossed into England, only to return at Christmas and attack Holyroodhouse, threatening to torch the place. It was almost certainly the intervention of some of the local citizens that saved the situation from getting completely out of hand. An attempt by Bothwell to kidnap James was botched; but not to be outdone, the earl descended once more upon Holyroodhouse, demanding a trial for witchcraft. Bothwell never got his trial. He left Scotland, and eventually died in poverty at Naples.

NORTH BERWICK, QUALITY STREET
1897 39176

The corner shop is long gone, but the clock tower remains.

NORTH BERWICK

LEFT: NORTH BERWICK, FROM THE LAW 1897 39183

Tourism brought with it a spate of hotel-building. The Royal was joined by the impressive Marine Hotel which had hot and cold running water.

ABOVE: NORTH BERWICK, THE LAW 1897 39175

North Berwick Law rises 612 ft above the town. On the summit is a watch-tower dating from the Napoleonic Wars, and an archway made from the jawbones of a whale.

BELOW: NORTH BERWICK, THE SEAFRONT 1897 39180

The popular seafront of North Berwick.

ABOVE: NORTH BERWICK, THE MARINE HOTEL AND THE LINKS 1897 39177

North Berwick's popularity as a resort began in the 1840s, but as late as 1859, when HRH The Prince of Wales visited the town, there was a serious lack of accommodation for tourists. The project to build a hotel somehow became involved with plans for a new gas works under the North Berwick Hotel & Gas Company.

North Berwick

North Berwick, The Bay 1897 39179

Here we see the broad sweep of the sandy bay to the west of the harbour area on a quiet day.

NORTH BERWICK

The Douglases were a powerful family: they were wardens of the Border Marches, lords of Galloway and skilled in war. By the end of the 15th century they controlled vast areas including Galloway, Lothian, Stirlingshire and Clydesdale.

North Berwick

One of the more interesting events in the history of this famous bird sanctuary occurred after the Battle of Killicrankie in July 1689. Despite defeating the forces of William III, the Jacobites failed to hold the advantage. One of the outcomes was that the Bass Rock was taken and held in the name of James VII from June 1691 to April 1694.

TANTALLON CASTLE 1897 39184

In 1388, the 2nd Earl of Douglas invaded the Earl of Northumberland's domain to the south. Douglas raided far and wide; then, after capturing Northumberland's standard, he returned home. On 5 August 1388, the two sides clashed yet again. In the savage hand-to-hand fighting that went on all night Douglas was killed, and the Earl of Northumberland was taken prisoner.

James V was resentful of the Douglases, so he laid siege to Tantallon in 1528. Red Douglas held out for three weeks before surrendering. Douglas went into exile in England, and his estates were forfeited to the crown.

Whitekirk

WHITEKIRK

The village and church probably owe their existence to the discovery of a holy well in 1294. Aeneas Sylvius Piccolomini (later Pope Pius II) came here during the reign of James I.

LEFT: WHITEKIRK, THE VILLAGE C1955 W3275002

A view of the village of Whitekirk.

BELOW: WHITEKIRK, ST MARY'S CHURCH C1955 W3275001

Here we see the 15th-century cruciform church of St Mary's, its massive tower surmounted by a wooden spire. The church was targeted by the suffragettes during a campaign of violence following the government's refusal to grant votes for women. Other targets for fire-bombing included Farrington Hall and Leuchars railway station.

BLACKBURN

S andwiched between Whitburn and Livingston, Blackburn in West Lothian stands on the River Almond. This selection of pictures were taken at the beginning of the 1960s.

BLACKBURN, THE CENTRE c1960   B7585008

A bleak featureless view of Blackburn New Town.

BLACKBURN

EDINBURGH

RIGHT: BLACKBURN, THE RIVER
ALMOND AND HOPEFIELD BRIDGE
c1960 B7585006

The River Almond flows into the Firth
of Forth at Cramond. A prophetess at
Cramond is said to have warned James I
of impending tragedy if he continued with
his journey to Perth. He was murdered.

BELOW: BLACKBURN, THE CENTRE
AND THE BOWLING GREEN c1960
B7585009

Typical 1960s structures span the whole
photograph. This was the typical layout of
a 1960s new town.

BLACKBURN, THE ALMONDVALE 'OLD FOLKS' HOME C1960 B7585002

Again, this building is typical of the 1960s. Everything looks unused in this photograph, the 'Old folks' home looks unloved in as yet, and the trees seem to have been just planted.

BLACKBURN, THE SHOPPING CENTRE AND THE GOLDEN HIND HOTEL C1960 B7585004

The precinct is typical of a style that dominated redevelopment and new town schemes of the late 1950s and 1960s. Examples can be seen throughout the UK, many of them now looking the worse for wear.

BLACKBURN

BLACKBURN, THE RIVER ALMOND c1960
B7585005

The River Almond flows from Blackburn to the three towns of East, Mid and West Calder. It was at Mid Calder in 1556 that John Knox first administered Communion according to Protestant rites.

Index

www.francisfrith.co.uk

The Francis Frith Collection publishes over 100 new titles each year. A selection of those currently available is listed below. For latest catalogue please contact The Francis Frith Collection. **Town Books** 96 pages, approximately 75 photos. **County and Themed Books** 128 pages, approximately 135 photos (unless specified). All titles hardback with laminated case and jacket, except those indicated pb (paperback)

Available from your local bookshop or from the publisher

The Francis Frith Collection Titles (continued)

Lancaster, Morecombe and Heysham Pocket Album
Leeds PA
Leicester
Leicestershire
Lincolnshire Living Memoires
Lincolnshire Pocket Album
Liverpool and Merseyside
London PA
Ludlow
Maidenhead
Maidstone
Malmesbury
Manchester PA
Marlborough
Matlock
Merseyside Living Memories
Nantwich and Crewe
New Forest
Newbury Living Memories
Newquay to St Ives
North Devon Living Memories
North London
North Wales
North Yorkshire
Northamptonshire
Northumberland
Northwich
Nottingham
Nottinghamshire PA
Oakham
Odiham Then and Now
Oxford Pocket Album
Oxfordshire
Padstow
Pembrokeshire
Penzance
Petersfield Then and Now
Plymouth
Poole and Sandbanks
Preston PA
Ramsgate Old and New
Reading Pocket Album
Redditch Living Memories
Redhill to Reigate
Rhondda Valley Living Mems
Richmond
Ringwood
Rochdale
Romford PA
Salisbury PA
Scotland
Scottish Castles
Sevenoaks and Tonbridge
Sheffield and South Yorkshire PA
Shropshire
Somerset
South Devon Coast
South Devon Living Memories
South East London
Southampton PA
Southend PA

Southport
Southwold to Aldeburgh
Stourbridge Living Memories
Stratford upon Avon
Stroud
Suffolk
Suffolk PA
Surrey Living Memories
Sussex
Sutton
Swanage and Purbeck
Swansea Pocket Album
Swindon Living Memories
Taunton
Teignmouth
Tenby and Saundersfoot
Tiverton
Torbay
Truro
Uppingham
Villages of Kent
Villages of Surrey
Villages of Sussex PA
Wakefield and the Five Towns Living Memories
Warrington
Warwick
Warwickshire PA
Wellingborough Living Memories
Wells
Welsh Castles
West Midlands PA
West Wiltshire Towns
West Yorkshire
Weston-super-Mare
Weymouth
Widnes and Runcorn
Wiltshire Churches
Wiltshire Living memories
Wiltshire PA
Wimborne
Winchester PA
Windermere
Windsor
Wirral
Wokingham and Bracknell
Woodbridge
Worcester
Worcestershire
Worcestershire Living Memories
Wyre Forest
York PA
Yorkshire
Yorkshire Coastal Memories
Yorkshire Dales
Yorkshire Revisited

See Frith books on the internet at www.francisfrith.co.uk

FRITH PRODUCTS & SERVICES

Francis Frith would doubtless be pleased to know that the pioneering publishing venture he started in 1860 still continues today. Over a hundred and forty years later, The Francis Frith Collection continues in the same innovative tradition and is now one of the foremost publishers of vintage photographs in the world. Some of the current activities include:

Interior Decoration

Today Frith's photographs can be seen framed and as giant wall murals in thousands of pubs, restaurants, hotels, banks, retail stores and other public buildings throughout the country. In every case they enhance the unique local atmosphere of the places they depict and provide reminders of gentler days in an increasingly busy and frenetic world.

Product Promotions

Frith products are used by many major companies to promote the sales of their own products or to reinforce their own history and heritage. Frith promotions have been used by Hovis bread, Courage beers, Scots Porage Oats, Colman's mustard, Cadbury's foods, Mellow Birds coffee, Dunhill pipe tobacco, Guinness, and Bulmer's Cider.

Genealogy and Family History

As the interest in family history and roots grows world-wide, more and more people are turning to Frith's photographs of Great Britain for images of the towns, villages and streets where their ancestors lived; and, of course, photographs of the churches and chapels where their ancestors were christened, married and buried are an essential part of every genealogy tree and family album.

Frith Products

All Frith photographs are available Framed or just as Mounted Prints and Posters (size 23 x 16 inches). These may be ordered from the address below. From time to time other products - Address Books, Calendars, Table Mats, etc - are available.

The Internet

Already ninety thousand Frith photographs can be viewed and purchased on the internet through the Frith websites and a myriad of partner sites.

For more detailed information on Frith companies and products, look at these sites:

www.francisfrith.co.uk
www.francisfrith.com
(for North American visitors)

See the complete list of Frith Books at:

www.francisfrith.co.uk

This web site is regularly updated with the latest list of publications from The Francis Frith Collection. If you wish to buy books relating to another part of the country that your local bookshop does not stock, you may purchase on-line.

For further information, trade, or author enquiries please contact us at the address below:
The Francis Frith Collection, Frith's Barn, Teffont, Salisbury, Wiltshire, England SP3 5QP.
Tel: +44 (0)1722 716 376 Fax: +44 (0)1722 716 881 Email: sales@francisfrith.co.uk

---

See Frith books on the internet at www.francisfrith.co.uk

FREE PRINT OF YOUR CHOICE

Mounted Print
Overall size 14 x 11 inches (355 x 280mm)

Choose any Frith photograph in this book.
Simply complete the Voucher opposite and
return it with your remittance for £3.50 (to cover
postage and handling) and we will print the
photograph of your choice in SEPIA (size 11 x 8
inches) and supply it in a cream mount with a
burgundy rule line (overall size 14 x 11 inches).
**Please note: aerial photographs and
photographs with a reference number
starting with a "Z" are not Frith photographs
and cannot be supplied under this offer.
Offer valid for delivery to one UK address only.**

PLUS: **Order additional Mounted Prints
at HALF PRICE - £9.50 each** (normally £19.00)
If you would like to order more Frith prints from
this book, possibly as gifts for friends and family,
you can buy them at half price (with no
additional postage and handling costs).

PLUS: **Have your Mounted Prints framed**
For an extra £18.00 per print you can have your
mounted print(s) framed in an elegant polished
wood and gilt moulding, overall size
16 x 13 inches (no additional postage and
handling required).

IMPORTANT!

**These special prices are only available if you use
this form to order. You must use the ORIGINAL
VOUCHER on this page (no copies permitted). We
can only despatch to one UK address. This offer
cannot be combined with any other offer.**

Send completed Voucher form to:
**The Francis Frith Collection, Frith's Barn,
Teffont, Salisbury, Wiltshire SP3 5QP**

CHOOSE A PHOTOGRAPH FROM THIS BOOK

for **FREE**
and Reduced Price
Frith Prints

*Please do not photocopy this voucher. Only the original is valid,
so please fill it in, cut it out and return it to us with your order.*

Picture ref no	Page no	Qty	Mounted @ £9.50	Framed + £18.00	Total Cost £
		1	Free of charge*	£	£
			£9.50	£	£
			£9.50	£	£
			£9.50	£	£
			£9.50	£	£
			£9.50	£	£

*Please allow 28 days
for delivery.
Offer available to one
UK address only*

* Post & handling		£3.50
Total Order Cost		£

Title of this book . . . .

I enclose a cheque/postal order for £ . . . .
made payable to 'The Francis Frith Collection'

OR please debit my Mastercard / Visa / Maestro card,
details below

Card Number

Issue No (Maestro only)   Valid from (Maestro)

Expires   Signature

Name Mr/Mrs/Ms . . . .

Address . . . .

. . . .

. . . .

. . . . Postcode . . . .

Daytime Tel No . . . .

Email . . . .

Valid to 31/12/12

Can you help us with information about any of the Frith photographs in this book?

We are gradually compiling an historical record for each of the photographs in the Frith archive. It is always fascinating to find out the names of the people shown in the pictures, as well as insights into the shops, buildings and other features depicted.

If you recognize anyone in the photographs in this book, or if you have information not already included in the author's caption, do let us know. We would love to hear from you, and will try to publish it in future books or articles.

Our production team

Frith books are produced by a small dedicated team at offices in the converted Grade II listed 18th-century barn at Teffont near Salisbury, illustrated above. Most have worked with the Frith Collection for many years. All have in common one quality: they have a passion for the Frith Collection. The team is constantly expanding, but currently includes:

Paul Baron, Jason Buck, John Buck, Ruth Butler, Heather Crisp, David Davies, Louis du Mont, Isobel Hall, Lucy Hart, Julian Hight, Peter Horne, James Kinnear, Karen Kinnear, Tina Leary, Stuart Login, Sue Molloy, Sarah Roberts, Kate Rotondetto, Dean Scource, Eliza Sackett, Terence Sackett, Sandra Sampson, Adrian Sanders, Sandra Sanger, Julia Skinner, Miles Smith, Lewis Taylor, Shelley Tolcher, Lorraine Tuck, Miranda Tunnicliffe, David Turner and Ricky Williams.

Free Print – see overleaf